W9-BZG-219

Lakes

Diyan Leake

Chicago, Illinois

© 2015 Heinemann Library
an imprint of Capstone Global Library, LLC
Chicago, Illinois

To contact Capstone Global Library, please call 800-747-4992,
or visit our website www.capstonepub.com

All rights reserved. No part of this publication may be
reproduced or transmitted in any form or by any means,
electronic or mechanical, including photocopying, recording,
taping, or any information storage and retrieval system, without
permission in writing from the publisher.

Edited by Joanna Issa and Penny West
Designed by Philippa Jenkins
Original illustrations © Capstone Global Library Ltd 2014
Picture research by Mica Brancic
Production by Helen McCreath
Originated by Capstone Global Library Ltd
Printed and bound in China Leo Paper Group

18 17 16 15 14
10 9 8 7 6 5 4 3 2 1

Library of Congress Cataloging-in-Publication Data

Leake, Diyan.
  Lakes / Diyan Leake.
    pages cm.—(Water, water everywhere!)
  Includes bibliographical references and index.
  ISBN 978-1-4846-0450-2 (hb)
  1. Lakes—Juvenile literature. I. Title.

GB1603.8.L43 2015
551.48'2—dc23   2013039547

Acknowledgments
We would like to thank the following for permission to reproduce
photographs: Alamy pp. 6 (© Destinations by Evgeniya Moroz),
9 (© Art Directors & TRIP/Jane Sweeney), 18 (© Picture Partners),
19 (© MaximImages); Getty Images pp. 15 (Yves Marcoux),
16 (Stockbyte/altrendo images), 21 (The Image Bank/Neil
Beckerman), 22a (National Geographic/Jonathan Kingston);
Shutterstock pp. 4 (© Doin Oakenhelm), 5 (© Kevin Eaves),
7 (© Tatiana Grozetskaya), 10 (© feiyuezhangjie), 11, 23b (©
topseller), 12 (© Marco Regalia), 13, 23c (© Eric Broder Van
Dyke), 14, 23a (© Chris Geszvain), 17 (© Frank L Junior), 20 (©
DNF Style), 22b (© Kevin Eaves), 22c (© WayneImage), 23a (©
Chris Geszvain).

Cover photograph reproduced with permission of Alamy
(© Gavin Hellier).
Back cover photograph reproduced with permission of
Shutterstock/© Kevin Eaves.

We would like to thank Michael Bright and Nancy Harris for their
invaluable help in the preparation of this book.

Every effort has been made to contact copyright holders of
material reproduced in this book. Any omissions will be rectified
in subsequent printings if notice is given to the publisher.

All the Internet addresses (URLs) given in this book were valid at
the time of going to press. However, due to the dynamic nature
of the Internet, some addresses may have changed, or sites
may have changed or ceased to exist since publication. While
the author and publisher regret any inconvenience this may
cause readers, no responsibility for any such changes can be
accepted by either the author or the publisher.

Contents

Lakes

A lake is a large body of water.

A lake has land all around it.

6

Some lakes have mountains around them.

Some lakes have forests
around them.

Lakes of the World

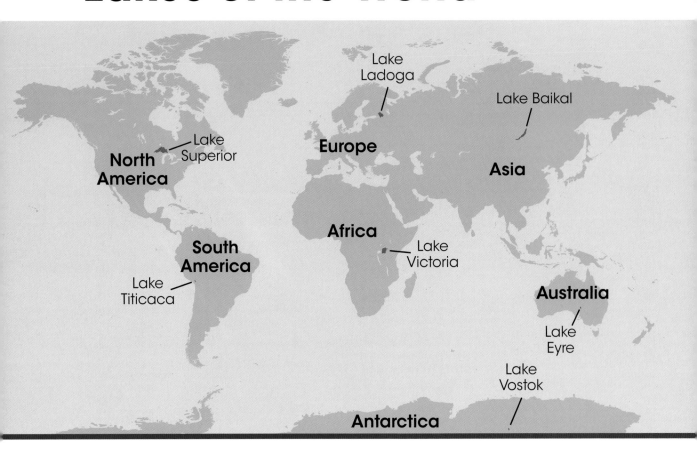

Lake
Ladoga

Lake Baikal

Europe

North
America

Asia

Lake
Superior

Africa

South
America

Lake
Victoria

Lake
Titicaca

Australia

Lake
Eyre

Lake
Vostok

Antarctica

There are lakes all over the world.

Here are some of the biggest.

Lake Titicaca is one of the biggest lakes in the world.

Freshwater and Saltwater

Some lakes have freshwater.

This means that the water is
not salty.

Some lakes have saltwater.

12

This means that the water is salty.

What Makes a Lake?

dam

 People make some lakes by blocking a river with a dam.

The water in a lake may come
from a river flowing into it.

15

How People Use Lakes

People enjoy being by a lake.

People can sail boats on a lake.

People need water to drink and wash.

Some of this water comes
from lakes.

19

Having Fun on Lakes

It is fun to spend time by a lake.

Stay safe! Always have an adult with you when you are near water.

Quiz

Which of these is a lake?

A

B

C

Answer on page 24

Picture Glossary

dam barrier to hold back water

freshwater freshwater is not salty

saltwater water that has salt in it

Index

Answer to quiz on page 22: Picture **B** shows a lake.

Note to Parents and Teachers

Before reading

Locate a local or world lake on Google Maps. Show the children a map view that includes the lake. Can they describe what they see on the map? Pointing to the lake, ask the children to explain what it is and what it is called. Ask the children to suggest what they might see if they were to stand on the shore of the lake. If street view is available, use it to find out what they would see.

After reading

• Arrange a visit to a local reservoir. Many reservoirs have education centers that support teaching and learning across a range of water-related themes, including water conservation, water safety, and the water cycle.

• Create a display backdrop showing a lake and the surrounding environment. The children could create labeled features to add to the display, such as a dam or a water treatment plant, people enjoying leisure activities, and living things on the shore and in the water.

Horsham Township Library

W9-BYX-224

FRANKLIN PIERCE COLLEGE

LIBRARY

JOHN C. SAMPSON

THE PUMPKIN PEOPLE

DAVID CAVAGNARO
AND
MAGGIE CAVAGNARO

Sierra Club Books/Charles Scribner's Sons
San Francisco/New York

A YOLLA BOLLY PRESS BOOK

Copyright © 1979 by David Cavagnaro and Maggie Cavagnaro

All rights reserved. No part of this book may be reproduced in any form or
by any electronic or mechanical means including information storage and retrieval
systems without permission in writing from the publisher. Trade distribution is
by Charles Scribner's Sons, 597 Fifth Avenue, New York, New York 10017.

The Pumpkin People was edited and prepared for publication at The Yolla Bolly Press,
Covelo, California, during the winter of 1978 under the supervision of James and
Carolyn Robertson. Production staff: Diana Fairbanks, Joyca Cunnan,
Carla Shafer, Barbara Speegle, and Dan Hibshman.

Manufactured in the United States of America

1 3 5 7 9 11 13 15 17 19 MD/C 20 18 16 14 12 10 8 6 4 2
1 3 5 7 9 11 13 15 17 19 MD/P 20 18 16 14 12 10 8 6 4 2

Library of Congress Cataloging in Publication Data

Cavagnaro, David.
The pumpkin people.
SUMMARY: A young boy watches as the seeds he plants in the garden
grow into a riot of colorful pumpkins and squashes and are carved
into jack-o'-lanterns with unique personalities.
1. Pumpkin — Juvenile literature. 2. Squash — Juvenile literature.
3. Jack-o'-lanterns — Juvenile literature.
[1. Pumpkin. 2. Squash.] I. Cavagnaro, Maggie, 1943-   joint author. II. Title.
SB347.C38 1979   635'.62   79-4032
ISBN 0-684-16109-5

CURR
49623
GT
4965
.C3
1979

*For the friends
who shared in the celebrations
at Bolinas Lagoon*

4

IN THE SPRING Pippin helped plant pumpkins. "Pointed end down," I showed him, handing him the seeds. "That's where the root will come out."

We put them in the ground near the winter squash where they would have lots of space to roam with their long, crawling runners.

Besides pumpkins, we planted seeds of many other kinds of squash. There were varieties from England, China, Africa, and very old kinds still grown by the Indians of Mexico and Central America. There were gourds, too, of many shapes, sizes, and colors.

Seeds are among the most magic things in the world. Each one is a package from which will grow a special kind of plant, and each plant will be just slightly different, even from those of its own kind. We grow almost all our food in the garden. Each year we are amazed at the quantity and variety of plants which come from just a handful of seeds. This year, however, we planted more than the seeds of squash. We planted the seeds of an adventure.

6

7

Summer days passed quickly in the garden. There was much watering and weeding to do. Pippin and his mother, Maggie, built a scarecrow so that the birds would think someone was working in the garden all the time. Each day the squash runners grew longer. Their bright orange blossoms opened every morning, offering pollen and nectar to the bees that Maggie kept in the hive on the hill.

Gradually the nights grew cooler and the days shorter. The corn stalks began to dry, the grape leaves turned brilliant yellow and red. The melons we had enjoyed in late summer were gone. In their place came crisp autumn apples, grapes, and a promise of persimmons.

9

Pippin and Maggie came with me one day to the squash patch to check on the harvest. The vines were beginning to wither. Soon the crop would be ready.

And then a strange thing happened to us. It was a feeling, actually, which caught us like a breeze. It came out of fond childhood memories of family gatherings and from deep instincts of tribal festivities in which our ancestors gave thanks for a good harvest. Somehow we knew that the time had come for a celebration. We set a date and invited our friends to the farm.

11

On the morning of the big day, Pippin helped me with the harvest. We picked all the squash and sorted them. We placed a pile of eating squash in the cellar for storage so that we could have soups, baked squash, and pies all winter. We saved out the small gourds and the Indian corn. We picked chrysanthemums and other autumn flowers from the garden and made colorful decorations for the tables. All the rest of the squash we piled up for carving.

13

14

Meanwhile, Maggie prepared the food. Soon the canyon filled with smells of bread baking in the oven, spiced apple cider simmering on the stove, and roast lamb browning over glowing coals in the fire pit. Later, our friends arrived and joined us in carving jack-o'-lanterns. The youngest children drew faces on their squash, and older people helped them do the carving. Each person worked on several squash, laughing over the expressions as they took form. Soon the completed jack-o'-lanterns made a big pile on the grass amid heaps of seeds and carvings.

Some of the jacks were long and skinny; others were round and squat. Some were green, some yellow, others orange. Each carver had given to his squash a unique personality. All the faces were different, one from another; together they looked like an audience of odd garden folk come to watch the party.

16

17

18

After most of the squash had been given faces, we gathered to-gether scraps of wood and built a variety of boats, some just large enough to carry a single jack-o'-lantern and others so big that there was enough space for several pumpkin passengers. Pippin and his friends, who were especially fond of boats, even built masts on theirs and rigged them with sails.

After the sun went down behind the ridge, we set half the squash people aside with the boats and arranged the rest near the house on a table and benches. Each one received a candle, placed inside beneath the lid.

As dusk approached, bats left their hiding places in the wall spaces and attic of the barn. We could see their dark forms against the sky as they darted about in search of insects. The time had come to launch the pumpkins.

We all gathered with our jack-o'-lanterns and their boats at the shore of the lagoon which lay just in front of the old ranch house. The evening was cool and crystal clear. A thin crescent moon joined the planet Venus on the horizon.

High tide was ebbing, and the water flowed gently through winding channels of the lagoon on its way back to the sea. One by one the pumpkins were lit, placed upon their boats, and set adrift in the current. Some of the boats tipped and sank under the weight of their passengers. But soon there was a long string of boats floating off into the gathering darkness, their glowing passengers staring back in silent farewell. Finally, we lost sight of them in the distance. We were sending our newly made friends away upon an unknown journey. We wondered what their adventures would be.

We walked quietly back to the ranch house. It was nearly dark now. A great horned owl, who nested each year with his mate in the forest nearby, flew to the top of an alder tree next to the garden. Its soft hooting drifted across the ranch yard, and we all listened.

21

We gathered around the remaining pumpkins. The air was still and crisp with an autumn chill. Several of us struck matches and lit the candles one by one.

We stood back in silence. As we watched, all the squash people came to life. At last, someone broke the silence and whispered, "I have the strangest feeling that I have seen them all before."

Lined up in front of us were congressmen, actors, generals, workers, and poets. In a way it was like looking in the mirror. Our own faces—laughing, crying, jeering, joking—stared back at us. Beneath the clear autumn sky, in the dark silence where only the owl called, we looked at the squash people and saw ourselves.

23

After the dishes were done, we cleaned some of the largest pumpkin seeds for roasting and placed all the rest of the pulp and carvings on the compost pile in the garden. Our friends bid us good night and left for home, carrying gourds and Indian corn with them.

The next morning dawned cloudy. A stiff wind blew out of the west. By evening the first big Pacific storm of winter was hard upon us, and the wind raged. Heavy rain pounded against the windows all night, and we could hear the storm surf roar against the shore beyond the lagoon.

When the storm was over, Maggie, Pippin, and I went out to look at the garden. The scarecrow lay flat on the ground, his gourd head cracked and hidden among the cabbages. We walked down to the shore of the lagoon to see what the storm had done there. To our surprise, we found a pumpkin staring up at us from the rocky shore of the channel. Shipwrecked and battered, it still smiled through the crashing waves as though it had thoroughly enjoyed the adventure.

25

26

As we explored the shore, we found another and then another cast up on the rocks, their faces draped crazily with seaweed. The pumpkin voyagers had come home. Before the morning was over, we had found nearly all of them. We found their boats, too, some still intact but most broken to bits where the storm waves had smashed them against the rocks.

We collected all the squash people and carried them back to the farm. We placed them on the compost heap so they would return to the soil along with the seeds we had put there before.

The days gradually grew shorter. Winter rains came more frequently, keeping us indoors by the warm fire. One clear day, however, when I was out doing chores in the garden, I happened to walk past the compost pile.

The faces were there just as we had left them, saints and devils all heaped together; but their expressions had begun to change, each in its own way. As the flesh of each softened and withered, some grew mellow, some fierce; some kept their wrinkled smiles and some lost hope. To congressmen and actors, generals, workers, and poets, one and all, old age had come at last.

29

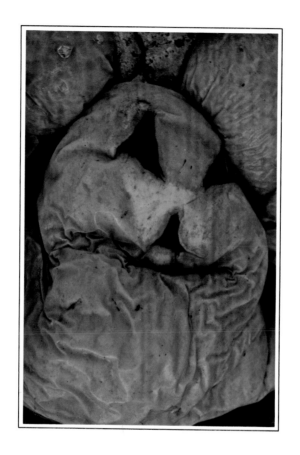

30

And then one day, as the last glimmer of life seemed to be ebbing from them, a wonderful thing happened. Pippin made the discovery. "Jack's coming back!" he shouted, running to the house from the garden. "Come see."

From the eye of one contented and happy old sage, a seed had sprouted. The story was about to begin again. From the sagging remains of one grand adventure had sprouted the seeds of another.

32

Franklin Pierce College Library

00064319

GT
4965
.C3

DATE DUE			
NOV 29 1982	NOV 17 '97		'97
FEB 17 '93			
MAY 25 1993			
NOV 85	27		
NOV 82 1994	OCT 22 2001		
	NOV 0 3 2004		
NOV 12 1994			
NOV 06 95	OCT 05 2011		
57 AON	OCT 21 2013		
OCT 3 0			

FRANKLIN PIERCE COLLEGE

LIBRARY

Rindge, NH 03461